MEN ALSO GET ABUSED

Men get abused too, discover how and the society's role in curbing it.

Dr. Peter Morrison

Copyright ©2022
Dr. Peter Morrison
All Rights Reserved

TABLE OF CONTENTS

INTRODUCTION

When it comes to domestic violence, most people conceive of women as victims and men as perpetrators. There is no denying that women account for the vast majority of victims, with men accounting for the majority of offenders.
An abusive female partner is still a possibility despite this. Domestic violence affects men just as much as it does women. Domestic violence is often underreported by victims, many of whom are embarrassed or humiliated to admit it. This makes it difficult to get accurate data. Due to the difficulty of quantifying non-physical forms of abuse, such as verbal, psychological, and financial, many people do not realize they are being abused at the time.

Every day, men of various ages and educational, socioeconomic, and cultural backgrounds are abused by their lovers. . Either their female or male partners abuse them, or they may have been exposed to domestic violence as a youngster in an abusive household.
As a man, as a result of your predicament, you're probably experiencing feelings of loneliness, embarrassment, and alienation. You're not the only one who's had this experience; it happens more often than you think, and it doesn't make you a weak person. Domestic abuse perpetrated against men often goes unchecked by the rest of society. Male victims are often

insulted or ignored. But even though many are
beginning to see this, more awareness and effort are
still needed.

CHAPTER ONE

TURNING A BLIND EYE

When it comes to male domestic abuse, why do we turn a blind eye?
Men's reluctance to bring up the subject of domestic violence has a variety of root issues. Male domestic abuse isn't spoken about in society since it isn't a taboo topic. When men stop talking about it, society as a whole will be less inclined to do so as well. Reporting abuse on men may be challenging for these reasons.

1. Women being abused is usually the focus of the society.

The treatment of women throughout history is consistent with the premise that men constitute the majority of the abusers. Long ago, males had complete control over their wives, so how can a person who couldn't vote just a few decades ago be the one who is abusing a person? Many public service announcements warn men against abusing their wives, but we've forgotten that men may also be victims.

It's a given that society expects men to refrain from hitting women, but the reality is that hitting anyone is unacceptable. When a woman slaps a man or pours her drink on a man, the society turns a blind eye and at best only gives out a loud exclamation, we're like "he's a man, he must have pissed her off and it's not going to hurt him anyway" and everyone just finds it amusing and maybe laugh about it, but when it happens the other way round, our reactions immediately turn into anger and disgust, " she must have pissed him off" definitely doesn't apply anymore and the man is immediately seen as a monster, a devil, an abuser, and other mean names.

This double standard is one of the major reasons men don't come out when facing abuse. This has to stop. The same standard has to be applied. Any form of physical assault should be treated with the same contempt irrespective of sex or gender.

Males abusing women is a common theme in the media. Due to the cultural preference for strong, masculine role models (in film and literature, as well as on social media), this is the usual projection (in Hollywood, literature, social media influencers, etc.). Due to long-held gender stereotypes, it's easier to depict a strong guy thrashing a weak female. It's " heartbreaking "to see a helpless man getting beaten up. we're used to hearing stories about males abusing women in our society. Sadly, history has shown that this is a real but unpleasant possibility.
But what about a woman who utilizes her power over a guy to her advantage? Surely, this implies that the man is naive and susceptible to persuasion.

men are frequently hesitant to come out about their abuse and seek treatment when they need it. This, of course, assumes that the victim is conscious of his situation.

2. Men do not believe that they are victims.
For those who have been abused, it is typical for them to be unable to recognize or acknowledge their abuse. When a man accepts that he's being abused in a relationship, it might make him feel less masculine and less like a real man. Thus, he may form psychological constructs—patterns of behavior or beliefs—to better understand and explain his experience.

Men's perceptions of what constitutes domestic abuse may also be skewed.
Abuse isn't always physical, but a man can mistakenly believe you're asking whether his wife hits him if you inquire if he's being mistreated. Emotional, mental, verbal, and sexual abuse are more likely to occur when someone is being mistreated.

Those who have been sexually assaulted by their partners sometimes fail to see that they have been subjected to other forms of abuse as well.
We don't know how pervasive male-on-male relationship abuse is because we have a cultural blind spot for it.

As well as distributing resources, domestic violence support groups must also educate the public and help men overcome preconceptions in order to recognize themselves as victims. we want the men to know that we care about their plight and sympathize with their plight.

3. Our society has a tendency to focus on physical abuse
Another reason we disregard the mistreatment of guys is because violence is generally represented physically. Television stories of women being found injured are entertaining, but the reality is far more complicated.
If you think domestic violence is exclusively physical (slaps, punches, etc.), you may miss the warning signs. Non-physical forms of violence, such as emotional or financial abuse, are prevalent in men's lives. Due to the increased obliqueness of violence, men are more likely to conceal it.

4. Stigmatization
 survivors of domestic violence may feel humiliated to be the "strong guy" who should be able to protect themselves against an abusive partner, particularly if the abuser is a woman. They may also be afraid to come forward since it implies admitting a same-sex relationship they aren't ready to divulge. Male victims of domestic abuse may also suffer prejudice from police or domestic violence shelters who are suspicious of their assault claims.

CHAPTER TWO

HOW MEN GET ABUSED

Women may be physically violent to guys, but it's not the only way they abuse them. Men may be subjected to many types of abuse, including:

VERBAL AND EMOTIONAL ABUSE

When a guy assaults a woman physically, he is considered furious, out of control, and morally repugnant. On the other hand, many males have been educated not to utilize their physical dominance over women in an aggressive way.
A woman who is abusive, on the other hand, may exercise this restraint by giving in to her fury or manipulative inclinations and verbally or emotionally attacking her partner. This mindset of "you can't touch me" leaves a guy unclear about what to do except accept and live with it.

ABUSE IN THE FORM OF SEXUAL MANIPULATION

Men are equally more prone to sexual coercion by women. As a consequence, rather than utilizing force to control a guy, a woman may use sex as a weapon. In this case, it may look like:

- Withholding sex in return for what she wants

- Forced genital squeezing is an example of covert sexual abuse.

It's possible that some guys may not regard this as abuse since they are more sensitive to sexual activities. Using anything, even sex, to try to dominate your spouse, however, could be considered abuse.

MENTAL ABUSE

Psychological abuse by women is also possible. Here are a few instances:

- Disrespecting the masculine figures in their lives.
- Undermining the man's self-esteem
- Making the man feel alienated and reliant

False accusations of adultery are made, family connections are strained, and financial control and influence over behavior — such as overspending — are exercised using any of these methods.

If a man has children, they may be used against him. This power is used by some moms to influence and alienate their children from their fathers. Could harm their relationship with their children by revealing faults and habits that may turn them against their father. Both the man in issue and the youngsters being exploited are the victims of this abuse.

Your partner is abusing you if she insults, belittles, or publicly humiliates you In the presence of your friends, neighbors, colleagues, family members, members of the public, or on social media. She seizes your keys and medications. In order to control and isolate you, they may make up a false accusation against you in front of your friends, colleagues, or the police officers on duty. There are other ways men get abused but the points stated above are some of the more popular ones.

CHAPTER THREE

WHY DO GUYS STAY IN ABUSIVE RELATIONSHIPS?

To put an end to a relationship, especially an abusive one is not an easy thing to do. It doesn't matter the gender, it still takes courage. If you've been secluded from friends and family, intimidated, manipulated, and controlled, or physically and emotionally beaten down, it'll be considerably more difficult.

You might believe you have no choice but to stay in the relationship because:

1. You are embarrassed.
Many men are ashamed of being abused, incapable of standing up for themselves, or having failed in their role as a man, husband, or father.

2. You think You must stay because of your religious views.
Divorce and separation are frowned upon in some religions. However, while religions do not always prevent divorce or separation in deserving circumstances, some adherents of such religions are often judgmental and enslaving. Some religious people may regard a man who admits to being mistreated as a

weak individual. He's supposed to be the " Head of the Home," but he's not even " manly" enough to rule his own home, so how can he lead a church department? One of the reasons a man can decide not to leave an abusive relationship is because of people who project their religions incorrectly.

3. There are insufficient resources.
 Many men are concerned that authorities will not believe them, that their abuse will be minimized because they are male, or that there will be few services available to support abused men.

4. You're in a same-sex relationship but are frightened of your partner outing you to your family or friends.

5 You're living in denial.
Denial of a problem in your relationship, much like with female domestic violence victims, will simply prolong the abuse. When your partner isn't abusing you, you may still love them and believe that they will change or that you can assist them.

The truth is that real change only happens when the abuser accepts the fact that they've done something wrong and then tries to get professional help.

6. You want to keep your kids safe.

You're afraid that if you leave, your spouse may injure or deny you access to your children. Obtaining custody of children is usually difficult for fathers, but even if you are confident in your ability to do so, you may feel overwhelmed at the prospect of parenting them on your own.

7. You're hoping for a change in your abusive partner. Abuse will very certainly continue. Abusers suffer from severe emotional and psychological issues. Change is not impossible, but it is neither quick nor simple. And change will only come when your abuser accepts full responsibility for her actions, seeks professional help, and stops blaming you, her miserable childhood, stress, work, alcohol, or her temper.

8. If you think you can assist your abuser... It's natural for you to want to assist your mate. You might believe you're the only one who understands him or that it's your job to solve his or her troubles. However, enduring and accepting recurrent abuse only serves to reinforce and enable the conduct. You're exacerbating the problem rather than assisting your abuser.

9. Your boyfriend has agreed to cease abusing you. When confronted with the repercussions of their actions, abusers frequently ask for a second opportunity, beg forgiveness, and pledge to change. They may mean what they say at the moment, but their ultimate purpose is to keep you under control and prevent you from

fleeing. Most of the time, once you've forgiven them and they're no longer afraid of you leaving, they soon return to their abusive conduct.

10. You're concerned about the consequences of your departure.
You may be concerned about what your abusive partner will do, where you will go, and how you will support yourself and your children. However, don't let your fear of the unknown keep you in a risky or harmful scenario.

CHAPTER FOUR

SIGNS THAT A MAN IS BEING ABUSED

So, how can you determine whether a man is being mistreated in his relationship if he doesn't want to talk about it and may not even recognize it — and there are no visible indications like bruises or broken bones? Men can, in fact, show indicators of abuse. You only need to know what to look for.

Consider the following signs which shows that a man is being abused.

1. Personality changes.
Any significant change in someone's personality should raise a warning signal. It doesn't always imply abuse, but it usually implies that something is wrong. A change in a man's personality, such as an outgoing person becoming withdrawn or responsible, or a steady man acting angry, wild, or irresponsibly, could indicate abuse.

2. Being worried or anxious about his partner's reaction.
It's unhealthy to be extremely concerned or anxious about how your partner will react to you on a regular basis. It could be a sign of apprehension that failing to please will result in punitive or abusive consequences. This is true for both men and women, and it can lead to a communication breakdown.

3. Apologizing excessively.
 A victim of abuse may become accustomed to making unnecessary apologies or over-explaining their actions.

4. Depressed mood. Men's depression often manifests as rage rather than a depressed mood.

5. Consumption of alcoholic beverages or other substances.
 Men are more likely than women to self-medicate with alcohol. They utilize it, as well as other narcotics, to cope with their feelings and escape. As a result, if a man begins to drink more than normal or begins smoking cigarettes or cannabis, take it as a clue that something is wrong.

6. Appearing to be sick in general.
 Men have a reputation for being unable to articulate their emotions. When a man is abused, he may not know how to talk about it, may feel ashamed of his condition, or may suppress his emotions. This can manifest itself as a visible sickness. In essence, he is becoming ill as a result of the torture.
Low self-esteem is number eight on the list. The loss of self-esteem is a consistent impact of maltreatment in both men and women. Especially if a man appears unsure of himself in an area where he was once

confident, he could be a victim of male abuse who has gone unnoticed.

These aren't the only indicators of male abuse, but they are among the most common. If you recognize these traits in yourself or a man you care about, it's time to take action.

CHAPTER FIVE

WHAT SHOULD MALE ABUSE VICTIMS DO?

REACH OUT FOR HELP.

Men who face abuse should not be reluctant to always reach out to their local domestic violence shelter, it doesn't really matter if it's a women-only shelter. If you feel it's Life-threatening, obtain advice from a domestic violence program or legal aid resource about getting a restraining order or order of protection against your partner and, if necessary, trying to get temporary custody of your children. Different legal advice will be given depending on each case.

NEVER RETALIATE.

Your partner who abuses you might try to get you angry so that you will retaliate or use physical aggression to fight back. Do not do it! It's part of your partner's plan to make herself the victim and turn the table against you. You might get arrested, jailed, removed from your home, separated from your children, etc and that might be probably what your partner wants. Keep your cool, it's very important you note this.

GET EVIDENCE OF THE ABUSE.

Ensure you keep sufficient evidence of all relevant incidents. Write them down and also record them. Arrange them properly into time, dates, witnesses, etc. Take pictures of injuries and recordings of threats. Get doctor's reports on injuries too. When you feel you have enough, you can create a copy and give it to the police for investigation. Make sure you have at least 2- 3 copies. One copy which will be readily available, another copy kept safely in a place only you know. Documents like passports and other important documents should be always within reach in case you need to leave the house for your safety.

PRACTICE SELF-CARE.

You should try joining a support group, and look for a mental health professional who is properly trained and equipped to treat traumas arising from domestic abuse.

LEAVE IF POSSIBLE.

Study the things that trigger your partner into abusive mode and note them. This should make you alert and ready in case of any violent escalation so that you will be in a good position to leave immediately. It's possible you might need to stay in order to protect your children, at this point, you should alert emergency services. As a citizen, whether male or female, it's your right to be protected and the duty of the police to do so.

CHAPTER SIX

MOVING ON

Putting a stop to abuse in any relationship and moving on is difficult and complicated. It would have been cool if it were so easy, but it's not. Ending a significant relationship is never easy. The decision is even more difficult when you've been detached from your family and friends, mentally exhausted, financially manipulated, and physically threatened.

If you are being abused, remember:

*You are not at fault for being abused or mistreated.
*You are not the cause of your partner's abusive behavior.
*You deserve to be treated with respect.
*You deserve a safe and happy life.
*Your children deserve a safe and happy life.
*You are not alone. There are people waiting to help.

The scars domestic violence and abuse leave behind can sometimes run deep. The trauma can stay with you for several weeks, months, or years after you've left that relationship. You may have PTSD, unexplained fear, trust issues, etc. But this is not something you face

alone. More than ever, you need your family, friends, and professionals to help you heal and move on. However, It can be done
The first step is usually to admit that as a man, you're being abused. It's usually a tough thing to admit but once that stage is crossed, then something positive can begin.

CREATE A SAFETY PLAN

Establishing safety is important. A safety plan can help you outline decisive actions you need to take to reduce the risk of harm or danger when you're trying to break away from the relationship. A safety plan may include:

- Someone trusted to contact for assistance or shelter.
- Important items to bring when leaving
- Steps to protect children and pets
- Steps to increase safety at work, school, place of worship, and stores.

BUILD A SAFETY NETWORK

To stop yourself from going back to your vomit, surround yourself with friends and loved ones who are abreast of the whole issue and who understand the reason you are

taking that step. There's this warmth gotten from loved ones.
Reconnect with loved ones, friends, and people in your vicinity, especially if you've been cut off from them during your relationship. Support from family and friends can help you move on from an abusive relationship.

CHANGE YOUR USER NAMES AND PASSWORDS.

 It's possible that your partner knows these sensitive details, if you think he or she can access your personal banking, email, social media, and other sensitive accounts, try to change your usernames and passwords. Even if you believe they don't have it, he or she may have guessed it, hacked your accounts, planted a bug or a spyware program to monitor your activities, and know your details. Ensure you Choose passwords that they won't think of. (Do not use your date of birth, nicknames, and other personal information).
As much as you can, without raising too much suspicion, don't let them have access to your computer, phones, and other gadgets.

REMEMBER WHY YOU LEFT

It's perfectly normal to miss an abusive partner, but that doesn't mean that it's right to be with them, Rather, it means that there was some good in the relationship, unfortunately, the toxic part outweighs the positives and you deserve a healthy, safe, progressive and exciting relationship.

Write yourself a note about why you chose to leave the relationship and why you feel it's important to not go back, this will serve as a reminder in case the thought of going back ever crosses your mind.

WORK TOWARD BECOMING MORE INDEPENDENT

 If your partner was responsible for your finances and shelter, you should find a safe space to live and a job can jumpstart your path to independence. Seek more financial freedom, including but not limited to sources of income, savings, and credit.
This may improve your chances of staying away from your partner or thinking about them.

THERAPY AND SUPPORT GROUPS.

Keep in mind that this isn't "couples counseling". therapy can help you build inner confidence, start new relationships, strengthen your existing relationships, set boundaries, and better understand the signs of a potential abuser.

A mental health professional and support groups can help to navigate the emotional recovery process in building healthier relationships. Knowledge, they say, is power. This can also help you heal.

CONCLUSION

BUILDING HEALTHY NEW RELATIONSHIPS

After the trauma of a toxic and abusive relationship, getting over the pain might take a long process, you probably want it to be over as fast as possible but don't skip or rush the process, it might take time to get over the pain and trauma but you can heal and move on.

After getting out of an abusive situation, don't be quick to jump into a new romantic relationship. I know you want to experience all the love, excitement, intimacy, and peace that true love beings but take it slow, take your time and heal first so that you won't be a toxic partner to your new lover and so that you won't fall into the trap of another abusive relationship.

www.ingramcontent.com/pod-product-compliance
Lightning Source LLC
Chambersburg PA
CBHW052138150726

48002CB00006B/2662